AF260920

To my husband and son, who've endured endless talk of camels, tents, and clay texture tests.
And to my family and friends, for their patience, humor, and faith in every new adventure.

ISBN 978-1-997874-31-7

Cooper, Jacqueline
The Camel's Nose / written and illustrated by Jacqueline Cooper.

1. Fairy Tales. 2. Camels - Fiction 3. Tents - Fiction 4. Juvenile fiction. I. Title.
Cataloguing-in-publication data provided by the publisher.

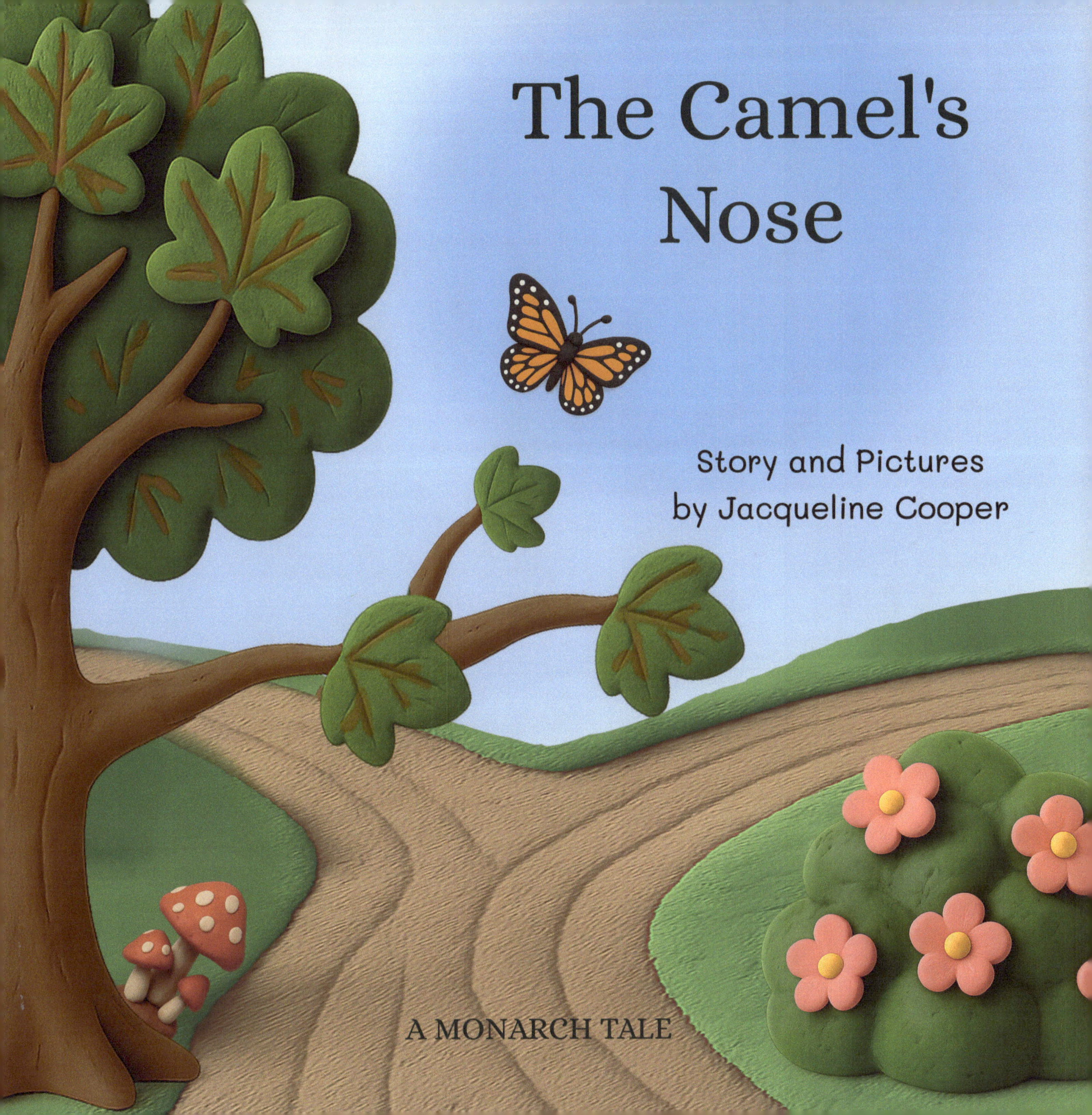
The Camel's
Nose

Story and Pictures
by Jacqueline Cooper

A MONARCH TALE

Long before there was a town called Maplebridge,
the world was full of stories.
This tale begins just as the day is ending.

A traveler lay down inside his tent.
The world outside was hushed and still.
Even the stars seemed ready for sleep.

Just as the traveler began to dream,
something stirred at the flap.
A nose slipped through the tent door.
"Good evening, kind traveler.
May I warm my nose inside your tent?" asked the camel.
"It's cold outside."

The traveler blinked sleepily.
"Yes, of course," he replied to the camel.
"You may warm your nose inside my tent."

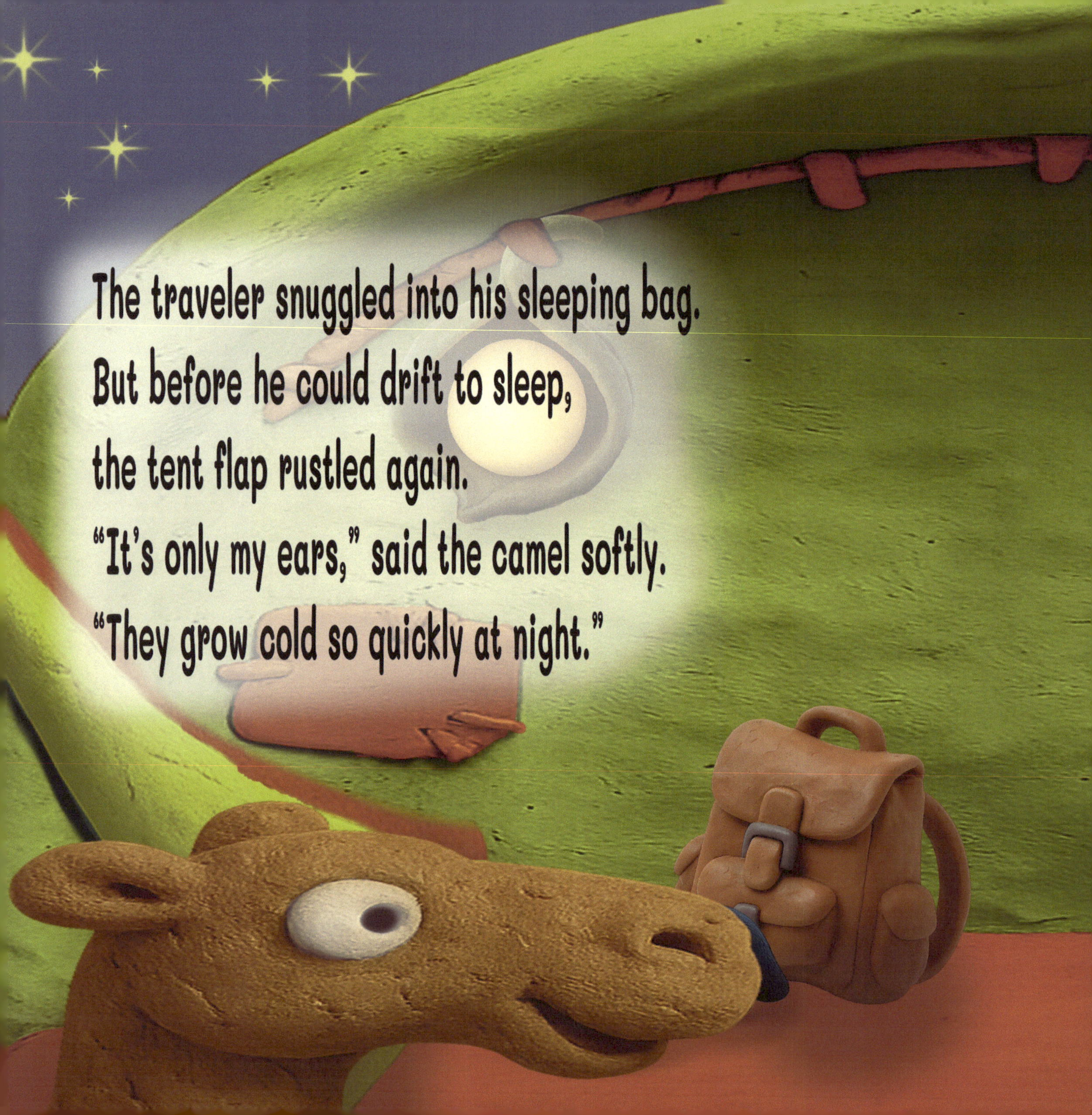The traveler snuggled into his sleeping bag.
But before he could drift to sleep,
the tent flap rustled again.
"It's only my ears," said the camel softly.
"They grow cold so quickly at night."

The traveler mumbled from under the sleeping bag,
"Yes, yes... warm your ears too."
The camel smiled and stretched a little further inside.

The traveler opened one eye and saw
that the camel's long neck had found its way inside.
"It's just my neck," whispered the camel.
"The wind is pretty chilly tonight."

The traveler, too tired to argue, made a bit of room.
"Okay," he agreed.
"Your neck may stay inside."
The camel nodded gratefully
and stretched its neck just a little more.

A leg slid through the flap of the tent.
"Just one leg," said the camel with a smile.
"It's cold outside."

The traveler lifted the backpack aside,
clearing the last bit of space in the tent.

A moment later, the camel's hump appeared.
"Just my hump," said the camel.
"It won't take up any space at all."

The traveler stared at the great hump filling the tent.

"Is there more of you out there?" he whispered.

"Well, yes," the camel replied.
"Naturally, like all camels,
I do have two back legs."

"Right," said the traveler slowly.
"Two back legs. Naturally."

"And finally, here's my tail," said the camel.

"So that's my whole body now."

The camel continued,

"This tent is really quite cozy, isn't it?"

"It is," agreed the traveler.
"Though I seem to have run out of room,"
he added, rolling up his sleeping bag.

"Oh! Perhaps if I turned around,"
said the camel, "there'd be more room?"
The traveler tried to stand out of the way.

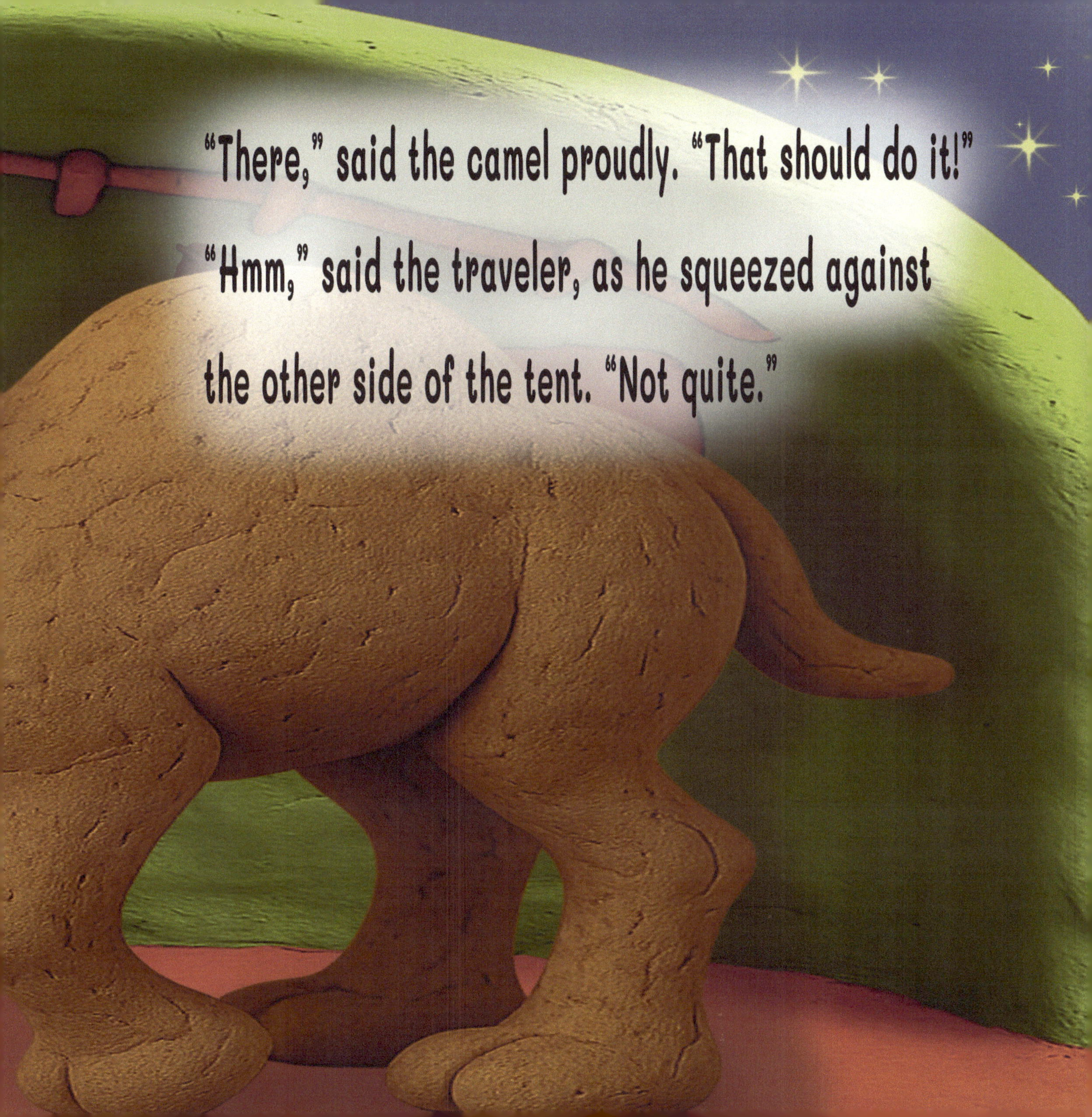

"There," said the camel proudly. "That should do it!"

"Hmm," said the traveler, as he squeezed against the other side of the tent. "Not quite."

"Maybe if I lie down," said the camel thoughtfully, "that might make more space."
The traveler backed toward the flap.
"If you think so," he murmured.

"At last," sighed the camel, curling his legs beneath him. "Now that feels just right."

The traveler nodded, then lifted the flap. "Sleep well," he said, as he stepped out.

The traveler finished packing up his camp site and walked away. "Next time," he thought to himself, "I will not give so much away!"

By morning, the clearing was still.
The traveler had gone,
a little wiser about how far kindness can stretch.

About this Tale

This story is based on *The Camel's Nose*,

a 19th-century fable often mistaken for one of Aesop's

because it shares the same concise, moral style.

First printed in English in the mid-1800s,

it has been retold for generations as a reminder

that small concessions can quickly grow beyond our intentions.

This adaptation was created for the *Monarch Tales* series from Little *Goodbyes Press*.